SALES MADE EASY

A *(Quick) Jump-Start Guide for Anyone*
Based on advice for introverts, from which everyone will benefit

Tarek Hassan

CONTENTS

Introduction 1

Why? 5

5 Ps of Selling 6

Introverts Underrated 12

Action is Magic 14

3 Quick Steps to Help You Sell Anything 16

Extras 26

Sales Made Easy

INTRODUCTION

I have somehow been in a sales function for my entire career. Every time I try to do something new, it doesn't quite work out and I'm put back into a sales role where I naturally excel.

I was never proud of being a salesperson, mostly because of the stigma of salespeople being annoying talkers who don't listen and just like to hear themselves spout off at the mouth. While this isn't true in the slightest, it has somehow come to be the perception of all salespeople and without segmentation of the different types of sales roles available.

Conversely, the most effective salespeople are great listeners who like other people. They see sales as a service to their fellow human with a chance to positively affect another person's life.

If you don't remember anything I've said here, please remember this one thing:

Sales is helping. Simple. The more you like to help others, the more naturally sales will come to you.

My first taste of sales was when I was 17. I didn't sell anything; I got sold. My father told me that they didn't have enough money for me to go to college, so I would need to join the army to qualify for the GI Bill to help us out.

Without second guessing this, I volunteered to go and talk to the recruiter that week. My father must have thought that was the easiest sale he ever had to make.

As I made my way over to the car and as my parents got in, there wasn't an ounce of nervousness on my part for some reason. Just like anything else in my life, I saw this as an adventure. You could say I was quite gullible in my younger years.

Once we arrived at the recruiter's office we discussed what my choices of jobs could be for the Army. Of course, my assumption (and we all know what happens when you assume – you make an ASS out of U and ME) was that he would guide me towards the best suitable position based on my interests and strengths. What a thought, right?

It turned out I was being led down a path that would make the recruiter the biggest bonus of his month, instead of something that would satisfy me long-term. As I was dreaming of becoming a fire fighter or something exciting like that, the recruiter tells me I'm a perfect fit for the food specialist role.

Food specialist? Of course, I start imagining myself as someone who could concoct great, creative meals. I was still quite surprised, as I'd never had anyone tell me that I would fit into a food service specialty before, especially by just looking at me for the first time. It was the way he told me this that made me think, wow, he must see something in me.

Funny, isn't it?

Without hesitation, I signed the dotted line to become a food service specialist for the US Army and to serve 6 years in the reserve, then two years in the independent ready reserve – which meant you wouldn't have to do anything unless there was a war in those two years and they could call you if they needed you for service.

It wasn't until much later, after going through boot camp and US army cook school, that my role would apparently turn out to be less glamourous than the way the recruiter pitched it to me at the time.

I ended up waking up earlier than everyone else, cooking eggs and "chili mac" for 300 or more people at a time, and then going to bed after everyone, sorely tired each day.

For me, it was the worst job I ever had. Because of this experience, I'm not a fan of being in the kitchen for more than 30 minutes to this day.

That was my first lesson in sales… being sold a "bill of goods". This is where I learned what sales should be and what sales shouldn't be. The goal is to help others, not hurt them.

I'm still not sure how I really ended up in sales or why I was natural at it. All I know is that I stumbled into it during college and never really strayed from the path since. My first sales job was working at a cart in the mall selling solid color t-shirts. It was an easy job. All I had to do was charm the customer with attention and see which color matched them the best.

At the time, I was more interested in selling myself to the girl who worked at the sunglass cart next door. Most of my time was spent hanging out with her and trying to find the right solution to win her over. I was persistent, to say the least. Unfortunately, I kept trying and failing, never giving up until I started dating another girl from school.

That's where I first learned that persistence would get you somewhere. It might not be with your first choice, but you'll be matched with the right person or opportunity with a little bit of work.

Relationships are all the same... the one you're looking for is looking for you as well! Take it easy but keep persistently moving forward.

WHY?

You're probably asking yourself, why do I care whether I can sell? I can just hire someone on my own, can't I? Short answer… yes, you could.

However, to lead your company (or to sell anyone on anything at any time), you will have to learn to sell and share your vision and value proposition at some point. You might as well start now. If you own your own business, the bonus is that you will save some money in the beginning. This is, of course, on top of your ability to sell talented professionals on joining your organization and helping you grow towards success. We're selling all the time, to many people…

How many times have you had to sell your wife or husband, your friends, your boss, or even your kids on your idea to get what you want?

Most people think that only sales professionals use sales tactics in everyday life. The truth of the matter is that we ALL use sales techniques all the time. It's just that some do it more than others.

Since we all need to use sales, we might as well learn what it takes to be good at it.

5 PS OF SELLING

I've been in sales professionally for 21 years now. In that time, I have read plenty of books and advice columns on how to persuade someone else on your ideas and desires.

Personally, I've found that many over-complicate the topic and put too much thinking in the process. This takes away from the natural approach to getting what you want from another person.

With the practical knowledge I've acquired, I have found that there are 5 traits you can master to help you get what you want; to close the deal with the person you are trying to persuade. Believe it or not, all five traits start with the letter P. This will hopefully make it easier to remember.

The five traits are Passion, Persistence, Proactivity, Product Knowledge, and a Pleasing Personality.

Enthusiasm is important as well, but since it doesn't start with a P, it didn't make the cut for this discussion. Luckily, enthusiasm usually stems from passion. If you want to sell something, make sure you're passionate about what you're communicating. The person you're selling to will sense your enthusiasm and will be that much more willing to listen to you.

Passion is the foundation of communicating what you want.

Without passion, you have a car without a driver. With passion, you will feel enthusiasm, as stated above, for the product or service you want to sell. You will gain the natural feeling of excitement and drive to communicate what you want.

In the dictionary, passion can be loosely defined as a powerful force pushing you towards something else. The beauty of this trait is that the feeling is usually contagious and transferred over to the person listening to you. This, in turn, creates the same feeling of desire and understanding with the other person.

Have you ever said no to a passionate person? If you have, I'm sure it wasn't easy to do. It's hard to say no to someone bubbling up with excitement about something.

Be persistent.

Have you ever heard someone say that persistence is key? That's because it really is. Without persistence, there's no sale. Without persistence, ideas fall short of reaching the point they're supposed to end up at.

Persistence means doing whatever it takes to keep going. Whatever the object, service, or idea that you're trying to sell, you must make sure to continuously promote it to the other person. You cannot give up. There are countless stories of how small ideas became big because of the persistence of the individual pushing them. Just because someone says no the first time doesn't mean they'll continue to say no the next few times.

In sales, you will hear NO many times before you hear a yes. In fact, that yes might even be from the same person that told you no the first time. The only way to be sure is to stay persistent with that person until they give you a solid yes.

Or they get a court order forcing you to stay at least 500 feet away. That's a joke, of course, but persistence cannot be overstated. The ability to not give up leads to you getting what you want – most of the time.

Proactivity. What is it? The dictionary states it's "Acting in advance to deal with an expected difficulty" or "Acting in anticipation".

Being able to identify and plan answers and feedback for the person you're trying to sell to is very important.

Proactivity allows you to figure out what the person might need before they say it. Proactivity allows you to create a solution for the other person before they even know they need or desire it.

This ability to act before the person requires you to act on their behalf is the reason so many sales take place; you're gauging a future need for that person. The act of proactivity also includes continuously providing a future service to that individual (via other products or services) before they ask. Without proactivity, you lose out on sales opportunities that could have otherwise existed.

The next very important trait is product knowledge.

Knowing the product (or service) that you're selling is a major factor in sales. The only way to confidently inform the other person of what you want them to buy into is to be ready to answer all questions about that product or service.

If you don't have the correct information, the other person might question your credibility when it comes to this certain request. You need to be the expert of your product or service to gain credibility. Without credibility, your chances of closing the deal are significantly reduced.

Make sure that you know what you're talking about. However, you also need to make sure that whatever you're trying to sell meets the demands of the potential buyer.

Finally, make sure there isn't anything else out there that could better satisfy the customer. Do your research on the product and make sure you know what makes it unique to the individual to whom you're selling.

Finally, the most important underlying characteristic that all successful salespeople have is being able to obtain or show a pleasing personality to the potential buyer.

Let's be honest: if you're not in it for the interests of the other person, nothing you do will work. You need to find a way to please the individual with friendliness and show them that you're trying to find a unique solution that fits their need. One way this can be done is simply by asking questions.

Ask the other person questions like "How can I help you today?" "Have you seen or heard about these products or services before? If so, have you thought about how they can help you?" Another is "What issues are you having that I can help you resolve?" or "What can I do to make this work for you?"

These are all examples showing you're interested in pleasing the person you're trying to sell to BY ASKING QUESTIONS (VERY IMPORTANT).

When you show interest in the other person, that person will become interested in what you have to say. If you have a pleasing personality, you will hardly ever fail – as long as you persist in showing it.

When you ask questions to please your customer, a very beautiful thing starts to happen, you uncover a benefit specific to the customer. Once you find that specific benefit offered by your product or service, you are pretty much headed towards closing a deal.

Bonus P: There's another word that starts with P which, like a foundation, underlies all the other Ps. Without this P, implementing the other Ps would be a tough task. This P is Positivity.

Always work on being and staying positive. A positive mindset will change your life. There will always be some reason or another to go negative. However, staying positive will lead to success. Really… it's your only path to success. Everyone likes a positive person. If the customer likes you, they will work with you and understand you have value to offer.

While every sale and every individual are different, these five traits will help you establish a higher success rate when looking to convince your wife, husband, friend, coworker, or client on any matter.

Sales is all around us. Even if our job or life description doesn't state the word sales in it, the need for sales is always there – whether we want it or not.

We might as well be good at it.

INTROVERTS UNDERRATED

Are you an introvert? Some estimates show that introverts could possibly make up over 50% of our population.

Introverts seem to have a knack for processing information internally when dealing with the outside world. This is as opposed to communicating while they process the information, as extroverts do. In most cases, although not all, this automatically makes introverts excellent listeners.

Do you want to know the secret to selling?

It's listening.

No, it's not talking, as many have come to believe. The ability to listen to the other person or client and uncover their needs is the biggest underlying success factor in selling. When you can listen intently to the other person and uncover a need with which you can help, you are that much closer to closing the deal.

If you listen to others, others will probably like, respect, and trust you more. If you are likeable in sales, you will be more likely to close the deal.

Which deal?

Any deal.

Hiring a talented employee, creating a long-term revenue relationship, signing the dotted line of a contract, and so on.

Introverts naturally have the ability and experience to sell anything. The more you listen, the more you ask the right questions, and the more quickly you can find the solution that leads to success.

ACTION IS MAGIC

What good is it to know a lot, but not act on that knowledge?

It's the same with selling. You have all the tools to get out there and succeed. However, without the proper courage to get off the couch and take those steps out that door, you won't be successful.

Action is the cure for fear and hesitation. You can come up with many reasons why you don't need to act at this moment, for example. Equally, there's only one reason to act at the next opportune moment: because it will get you one step closer to where you really want to be.

Sales is an action-oriented process. You need to proactively reach out to someone, hopefully your intended target, to create a conversation and establish a rapport. Only then may you show that you are someone who will listen effectively and positively help them (or sell to them, same thing).

Selling is helping.

Take Action; get out there and create a relationship with someone. Help them.

If you help someone by being the first to take action, you also help yourself. The key is to first help the customer with their goals, then get them to help you with yours.

Give… then get!

Everyone wins. The result is a mutually rewarding relationship. This is the only way to sell correctly, positively, and continuously.

3 QUICK STEPS TO HELP YOU SELL ANYTHING

STEP 1 - FIND THE DECISION MAKER

There are certain steps towards accomplishing your goals in the sales process.

A great salesperson will use their experience and apply it to the company or person they're prospecting. But, before that can be done, they need the most important factor – who is the decision maker (also known as the DM) in the company; the person to whom they will sell their product or service.

This person can be the VP of Marketing, the CEO, the VP of Sales, the Director of Product Development, etc. It depends on which department you're looking to get into.

If you don't have the proper decision-maker, you don't have a chance. Anyone other than this person will be a waste of your time.

Finding the DM is easily done with the Internet. These days, anyone you're interested in is already somewhere on the Internet. In fact, there's probably a 99% chance that they have a website for their themselves or their company.

This is the quickest and best way to learn all there is to know about the company or person.

The Internet can be an easy, quick research tool if you're using it in a focused manner, or a long, painful process if you're not.

When you have a prospective company in mind, research the site. You can pretty much always guess the company's web address using their name and adding a dot com ending. For example, the Gap would be Gap.com, Sears would be Sears.com, etc.

If that doesn't work, then just go to Google or any other search engine and type in the company's name. You will get the company's website through the search results 9 times out of 10.

After finding the company's website, you'll see all the links to learn about them. If, for some reason, the DMs are not included as one of the links, you can always go to Hoovers.com and type in the company's name. This will bring up the company's executives, for example.

Find the most senior person in the department you're trying to target.

Do you want to create a marketing partnership with another company? Then find the executive in charge of the marketing department. If they aren't your contact for your proposed goals, then have them forward you to the appropriate person in that department who will help you.

Start as high as possible, not low…

This is what sales professionals know for a fact. Now you do too!

After you've found the DM of your prospective company, then comes the process of figuring out their email address – the most powerful tool you have in acquiring a meeting.

Note: Linkedin.com is also a great resource for this step

STEP 2 - EMAIL "CODE-BREAKING"

What's their email address? I sure would love to contact them.

Ever felt like this? Me too – we all have. This chapter will explain how you go about getting the email address of the DM you are trying to contact.

This is the most important step in the entire process because, without this, you cannot be proactive.

Email is the most powerful tool you and I can use to get hold of a powerful company executive. One thing you can count on is this: Even company executives check their email. They might not answer the phone, open their mail, pick up the fax, or check their voicemails, but they DO CHECK THEIR EMAILS!

One thing I've learned from past experience while using email is that almost every employee's email address is formatted the same within the same company. 9 times out of 10, the executive or DM you're trying to get ahold of has the same format as the entire work force in the same company, including the CEO!

Let's create the scenario of a job applicant, just as an example, to show how this process will work. In this example, we'll use "Bob."

Bob is applying for the "Product Manager" position for "Company AB". Bob is somewhat experienced in product management from his last company, even though his title was "Business Development Associate." Just as well, this new position is the position of his dreams.

By doing research on the website and contacting the front desk, Bob has already found out the company's information and its decision makers within the different departments. He found that the Product Manager position is under the Product Development department. Product Development has a Vice President as its head; this is the DM.

This DM happens to be "Lucy Powers." She is the highest person within this department. Lucy is the person Bob will email with his resume and professional reference letter.

Unless you were lucky enough to find out the DM's email address via a call or by researching the website, you will have to be creative in sending the email to the proper address. It's very easy. In the "to" section of your email, you will have to put as many combinations as possible of that person's name before the @ sign in the email.

In this case, Bob knows two things for sure. 1) The DM is Lucy Powers and 2) the company's website is www.companyab.com. 9 times out of 10, the company website is also the company's email server domain (@companyab.com).

From here, Bob can format his cover letter in the body of his email and attach his resume and professional reference letter(s).

In the "subject" line, he will put "Product Manager position" or Job # (if there's a job # under the listing on the website). In the "to" line, since he doesn't know her email address directly, he needs to include every professional email name format he can think of before the company's URL of @companyab.com.

He should come up with something that looks like this:

lucy.powers@companyab.com lucypowers@companyab.com

lucy_powers@companyab.com

lucyp@companyab.com

lpowers@companyab.com

This way, he covers all the main, professional formats of email addresses used by 99% of the companies out there now.

Of course, 1% of the time, you will see that some

executives don't use any of these formats or even the domain (@companyab.com). They might use:

lastname.firstname@

lastname.firstinitial@

lastinitialfirstname@

firstinitiallastinitial@

etc.

Or some companies might use a totally different domain

name for the email server. Most of the time this not the case, but in cases such as these, you might have to do more investigating over the phone.

If the front desk attendant won't give you the email and won't transfer you to the DM, ask to be transferred to the DM's assistant. Tell the assistant you would like to send her an email and ask that she forward it to the DM. 9 times out of 10, whatever email domain and format she gives you will be the same as the DM's email.

At this point, if you still can't get the DM's email address, just forward it to the assistant since you've already asked her nicely. 9 times out of 10, they will do this for you.

Once the email has been sent, depending on your email server, you will get back a message saying "undeliverable" or "unknown host" or something else to tell you that your email didn't reach ALL of its destinations.

This is good.

Once you open that email and see which email addresses it didn't reach, you can rule out those email formats for the DM and probably everyone else in the company.

As in this example, Bob might get an email back saying "undeliverable" in the subject line and the body saying listing these addresses:

lucy.powers@companyab.com

lucypowers@companyab.com

lucy_powers@companyab.com

lucyp@companyab.com

So, by process of elimination, Bob knows that Lucy's email is lpowers@companyab.com and that she received the email he sent.

This is a great confirmation for you, as well as the entry point into a new period of excitement as your know your intended recipient has received your information!

And as a quick note, most of America's top companies today use one of these three formats for their company emails:

firstname.lastname@

firstname_lastname@

firstinitiallastname@

STEP 3 – FOLLOW UP PHONE CALL AND THANK YOU!

After you've sent your email, wait one business day. If you haven't heard from them, follow up. In this case, Bob will call and ask the front desk attendant if he can talk to Ms. Lucy Powers.

9 times out of 10, because of her position, the front desk attendant will forward Bob to Ms. Powers' voicemail (or assistant) instead of to Ms. Powers directly.

So, Bob will leave a message enthusiastically and passionately explaining how he is very interested in this job and how he looks forward to discussing it soon.

Don't be afraid of this step; the people in these positions love persistence. That's the key to getting what you want, as it is while trying to sell any product to any company.

If you still haven't heard back from the DM a week after you sent the email (five business days), then it's recommended you call the DM again. If she has an assistant, find out when the DM will be back and if she can get the DM to call you.

GREAT assistants are always looking to help; that's why they're there. Remember that! If there's no assistant, leave another message for the DM.

At that point, space your calls to every two to three days. You want to be persistent, but not annoyingly so. Trust me, a real leader will take your calls in a positive manner.

Actually, a real leader would have gotten back to you in two days, which will probably happen 70% of the time.

Give it a try, you'll see!

The key to this step is persistence. You have to be persistent until they give you a solid "yes, let's move forward", or a solid "no, sorry, not now" or "we're not interested", for example.

These 3 steps are the only tools you need in starting the sales process.

Simply put, this is the sales process summarized and applied to the job search above.

This is the same technique that sales professionals use in their daily procedures, not to mention other areas of their lives. It works for them and it will work for you!

EXTRAS

What I learned that made me a better salesperson:

Sales is a great tool to use every day in every aspect of your life. I've been in sales for over 20 years and I have learned (through mostly minor, but also some major mistakes) what to do, what not to do, what actually works, and what really doesn't work.

The depiction of salespeople that you normally see online or in movies isn't representative of what a real, productive salesperson is like in real life.

You've probably seen the ego and the competition and the "whatever it takes" type of attitude to closing a sale (with ethics put on a back burner). In real life, those types of behaviors don't help increase sales. They help you out of a job quickly.

People Are Smart

What you need to remember is that people are smart. I learned this early and it was reinforced over time.

What I found was that the way I was raised was a proper preparation for success in sales and business type relationships – long-term and successful business relationships, to be clear.

When you respect your client as a human and you respect their time, their budget, and their goals, you also respect yourself and your approach to closing a deal with a person or an organization.

Humans, on a basic level, like to be respected and they like to be independent. They like to buy and not be sold. They like to do a great job. They like their boundaries and they like others who understand these basic rules of human behavior.

Clients Are Like Me

What I learned is that clients – and other people in general – are basically like me. If I use my time to listen and understand the other person by properly putting in the attention and respect, they deserve and desire, they will very much appreciate this behavior.

Thus, they are more willing to understand my position, to give me the attention I need, and to see me as trying to help them instead of trying to "trick them". Which should never be done, obviously.

Many clients will have reservations over working with salespeople. This may be because of past experiences with unethical types of salespeople.

Thus, your job as a salesperson is to show them that you understand; you are human, just like them, and you are only there to help.

If you can't offer them any value, then you need to move on and not take up that person's time again.

Finding A Human Connection

People are generally smart. If they're functioning, working adults, then they have likely been burned or hurt already.

Our job as sales professionals is to connect, enjoy the relationship, learn about our clients, and help them as much as necessary. Sometimes that means listening more and talking less.

Remember, you aren't the only person to approach this person. Make it real, make it memorable, and keep it human.

How To Be A Better Leader: Leaders Vs. Non-Leaders, The Difference

If you're a better leader, you will be a better salesperson.

Over the years, specifically the last 20, I've seen a big distinction between leaders and non-leaders. It's important enough to point out.

Humans have growth potential. If we're learning and growing, it helps to have leaders who empower others who come after them (the young, the new, and the learning) with their experiences.

While everyone else looks inward to better themselves, I believe leaders in outside society are important too. We have all seen or worked with a leader. At some point, we have also seen or worked with a non-leader.

There's a difference. If the goal is to grow positively and to be surrounded by like minds, I believe showing the distinction will help everyone grow in a more healthy, positive, empowering, and mutually beneficial way. I hope this is helpful.

So, what's the difference?

A leader grows your mind – a non-leader looks to control the mind.

A leader has value to offer others – a non-leader hasn't yet found a value to offer others.

A leader is courageous (through fear) – a non-leader is scared.

A leader empowers you – a non-leader holds you down.

A leader creates a positive vision for all – a non-leader creates "us vs them".

A leader is helpful – a non-leader is toxic.

A leader gives – a non-leader takes.

A leader teaches – a non-leader bullies.

A leader is open and inviting – a non-leader is closed.

A leader appreciates others – a non-leader is threatened by others.

A leader lifts others up – a non-leader squashes others.

A leader grows – a non-leader is set.

A leader moves everyone else forward – a non-leader holds everyone else back.

Note: I believe a non-leader can unlearn, learn, and be a leader.

Examples of Leaders:

The teacher who empowers her students.

The helper who helps others out of tough situations.

The entrepreneur who creates vision, positivity, communication, and an inclusive team.

The creator who changes things for the better for others.

The boss who appreciates you as you do them.

The friend in your life lifting you up.

That leader in society bringing humans from all backgrounds together towards positive growth.

You.

While we ourselves lead or aim to become leaders, I say we should balance it and surround ourselves with leaders on the outside as we move towards betterment. What do you say?

To growth, happiness, self-love, fulfillment, congruence with the self, and positive service and contribution to others.

<u>Great Questions you can use to find out more about your potential customer (Hint: open ended questions are the best!)</u>

1. What are your goals this year?
2. What keeps you up at night?
3. What have you seen work for you before?
4. How can I make your life easier?
5. Have you considered using _____? (Something regarding your product/service/industry)

6. Are you open to _____?

7. What are your responsibilities? Do you make these decisions on your own, or with others?

8. How can I help?

A First Email Template Below to Help You Get Started

First Email Option 1

Note: To place in the body of your email

Hello [Here you put the name of the Decision Maker who overlooks the department you are looking to connect with],

First of all congratulations [the company name - you are congratulating them on the great company they currently work for]! [Here you write in something positive that applies to the company and which you think is just amazing, or great, or of special interest, or unique, or a coincidence to you as well - the goal is to connect/tie you in closer to the decision maker and their company and to customize the letter to them only].

I am writing your today regarding [why are you writing them today].

[ask them a question regarding their business here where you know you can help with the answer]

Sales Made Easy

I wanted to reach out to you and let you know that we are engaging with [state their industry here] like yourself to help you [state here how your company will help theirs] through [your product]. With this [your product or service] you can [how this will benefit them]. Further, with this [product or service you are proposing to them] you can better [how will this help them in a much better way] and more...

We would be interested in piloting [your product or service] with you to show you the value it brings [their company name]. [note: if you don't have a pilot project, just leave out that sentence and place this instead – "We would be interested in showing you briefly how our product or service will bring you great value"] Do you/your team have just 20 minutes of time this week or next week to see a quick demo?

I know you will see the benefit and value to your company quickly.

Thank you for your time and I look forward to hearing your thoughts.

First and Last Name

Company Name

City, State

Phone Number

PS: If you feel more comfortable using other words anywhere in the body of the email feel free to use them as you see fit. The idea is that you use the basic outline.

Some Email Subject Lines You Can Use:

1. (Pose a relatable question). "Have you seen the _____?"

2. "Can we connect briefly? Mutually beneficial opportunity"

3. "_____ (put their company name) and _____(put your company name) – Perfect Opportunity Now!"

4. "Reaching out about a Mutually Beneficial Opportunity (1 min read)"

5. "Referred to you by _____. Great opportunity to work together now!" (If someone referred you to them. It's great leverage, use it).

6. (Something that connects you both after you researched their site which you can help them with, with your value/product/service) Ex. "Helping you with your teen driver presentation program. Perfect Timing!"

7. "Are you looking to _____? I can help"

8. "_____ (their company name) and _____ (your company name) – We have many contacts in common!"

9. "Mr. Morgan: Why other insurers are working with us now!" (put the person's name in the subject line to get his/her attention quickly)

10. "Great looking website! Have you considered _____?"

11. "Your Next Step for your Business – I can help (5 years of experience in successful implementations for others)"

12. "We have a lot in Common Mr. Morgan (1 min read)" Relating to them and quick.

13. "Special Promotion for _____ companies like yours – I can help Mr. Morgan"

14. General Advice: Create the email subject line <u>from you</u>. <u>Customize it with some targeted value to them by being you and showing your value too</u>. Keep it short when possible. Ex. "Your Services Package is an Industry Leader – I have helped many get the word out" or "Growing Your Reach – Why Others Have Worked with Us" (and show some testimonials).

Tarek Hassan

There are several ways you can present yourself in the subject line. My best advice is to just try different sentences to grab their attention, and see what works best for you. Trial and error is always the best way forward. Every contact is different. Every business is different. See what works best for you.

Sales Made Easy

If you want to learn more about the entire sales process in detail, you can see my "Sales System for Anyone" product and service, on Gumroad. It will give you all the tools you need to start and close a sale from beginning to end, including templates, a cadence sheet, and an entire sales system explained.

Here is the link: https://gumroad.com/l/myjumpstartsales

If you have any questions, please message me on-

Twitter @postivetarek

or email me anytime at jumpstartjourney@gmail.com.

Good luck and happy selling!

Tarek Hassan

https://gumroad.com/jumpstartjourney

www.jumpstartjourney.com

Tarek Hassan © 2021 All Rights Reserved

www.ingramcontent.com/pod-product-compliance
Lightning Source LLC
Chambersburg PA
CBHW040254220526
45473CB00001B/479